Tax Strategies for High Net-Worth Individuals:

Save Money. Invest.
Reduce Taxes

By: Adil N. Mackwani

MBA, Series 6, Series 63, Series 65

Copyright © 2020 Adil N. Mackwani.

All rights reserved. This book or any portion thereof may not be reproduced or used in any manner whatsoever without the express written permission of the publisher except for the use of brief quotations in a book review.

First printing, 2020.

Publisher

M&A Wealth

5003 Collingwood Court

Sugarland, TX 77479

www.mandawealth.com

info@mandawealth.com

This book is written for every individual in pursuit of the American Dream.

Keep Dreaming and Keep Learning!

About Adil Mackwani

Adil N. Mackwani was born In Houston, Texas to an immigrant couple who are proud Americans that worked hard to create the American Dream. Growing up, talks around the dinner table would revolve around the businesses that his family owned. He saw how hard his parents were working and wanted to figure out instead how to make their money work hard for them. This led Adil to develop a passion for business and to study capital markets. His interest in business led him to be elected as President of DECA at Clements high school. Adil then went on to attend the University of Texas and then continued to pursue an MBA in Finance and Investment Management from the University of Houston.

Throughout his studies he began to read and educate himself on teachings of value investing and financial planning. Which led him to begin his career at a Boutique Financial Planning firm in Houston. Over the years he worked with business owners and individuals to educate them on how to achieve financial freedom while growing their assets. Adil formed M&A Wealth to create more value opportunities for his clients while giving a personalized approach to financial planning that focuses on the goals of businesses and individuals.

Table of Contents

About Adil Mackwani iv

Preface 1

The Basics: Emergency Funds 2

Cash Value Life Insurance: Thinking Like A Bank 7

HSA Accounts: Triple Tax Savings 12

Tax Deferred Accounts 17

Roth IRAs And 401(k)s 24

Backdoor Roth IRAs: Roth Accounts At Any Income Level . 29

College 529 Plan Savings 34

Mega Backdoor Roth Accounts 39

Non-Qualified Deferred Compensation Plans 44

Why You Need A Regular Brokerage Account 49

Deferred Annuities 54

Long-term Care Insurance 59

What To Do With Social Security In Retirement 64

C Corporation Tax Advantages 69

Dynasty Trusts: What They Are And Why You Might Need Them 77

Which Tax-Advantaged Accounts Should I Open First? 86

2020 Tax Law Changes You Need To Know 91

Conclusion 96

Preface

When websites and books discuss retirement strategies, many of them come from a perspective of helping average people save money. While this perspective has value, this advice frequently doesn't have the depth required for high net worth individuals. People who are earning well into the six figures and have net-worth's that are at least six figures, and maybe even seven, have significantly more retirement planning opportunities available to them. For example, high net worth people need to consider trusts and using corporations to shelter money from taxation. Most articles online won't talk about this.

I wrote this book as a guide for minimizing tax and saving for retirement for a high net worth person. After reading this definitive guide, you will know many of the methods and account types that you can use to save money efficiently for retirement.

Of course, you may not need to (or be able to) open all the accounts listed within this e-book. However, you will at least have exposure to them so you can understand if they are a good fit for you. This is for informational purposes only. Please Consult an advisor before making any decisions.

Without further discussion, let's get into our first topic!

The Basics: Emergency Funds

When many people start their careers, they often become focused on saving for retirement. They walk into their company's benefits presentations and see all the plans that they need to invest in to defer taxation. 401(k)s, IRAs, HSAs, and accounts like them are all fantastic vehicles for deferring taxes. You need to be investing in those to have a comfortable retirement.

However, many times, these investments come at a cost. Individuals are putting so much money into these funds that they aren't focusing on building an emergency savings account. Having an emergency savings fund means that you can pay for your day-to-day expenses without needing to touch your retirement savings. While this might not seem super important when you are employed (since you have regular paychecks), there are many situations in which you might need an emergency fund.

Job Loss

Being laid off is an unfortunate possibility for the vast majority of working Americans. Even if you are a highly-compensated employee, there is still a possibility of losing your job. While the current economy is relatively robust and opportunities are plentiful, it will always take time to find new employment. A typical job search can last for six months to a year. That timeframe can be even longer depending on what type of jobs you're seeking (there aren't too many director spots open at Fortune 500 companies, for example).

Unexpected Expenses

Did the roof start leaking? Did you come home one night and a water pipe has burst? Did you break your leg while vacationing in another state, and that hospital is out-of-network? Unexpected expenses happen all the time. You cannot plan for what they will be or when they will be, but you do know they are coming.

If you are a homeowner, these expenses can run in the tens of thousands pretty quickly. Medical bills can also be significant. If you are married and your partner falls ill and can no longer work, you may need to plan on being on one income stream for a while.

Business Downturn

If you own a small business, not only do you need an emergency fund, but your business needs one as well. Recessions and other slowdowns will invariably happen. There will also be cash flow crunches where loans and other payments will be due before your accounts receivable payments come in. During these times, you need a cushion to keep both you and your business afloat.

How Much Do You Need To Save?

An emergency savings fund is essential. "6 months worth of expenses" is a phrase that gets thrown around a lot. You have likely heard that advice before. While that advice is well-intentioned, it doesn't convey the whole story.

For a highly-compensated employee - someone, say, making $500,000 per year - having six months' worth of expenses could mean having $100,000 just sitting in a bank account. That $100,000 in money would be earning 1% in interest ($1,000 per year) instead of the 5% or more ($5,000+) that it could be making in other equity types. There's a significant opportunity cost to having this much money sitting in a bank account.

In reality, what you typically want to do is create two emergency funds. The first fund is for short-term expenses. That account is a bank account or a money market account since it provides high liquidity. Ideally, it should contain two to three months' worth of expenses. The idea is that you can draw from this fund to pay for any immediate needs. For example, if you lose your job, you can use this money to pay your bills until you're able to sell some other assets.

The second fund is for long-term expenses. This money should be in a standard brokerage account. In this account, you should have at least six to nine months' worth of expenditures, but many advisors say to have one year's worth or more. You would invest this money, just like everything else, except that you would make sure that all your investments were reasonably liquid. You would not be putting this into CDs and other investment types that may take a year or more to mature.

Business owners will need to think a little bit longer-term. It's easy to have a downturn in business that lasts more than six months or a year. Ideally, business owners should have around 18 months of emergency funds to be able to ride out recessions and other natural market cycles.

For someone whose monthly expenses are $10,000, the ideal scenario would be between $20,000 and $30,000 sitting in a bank account and between $60,000 and $120,000 in stocks and other higher-returning investments.

Should You Stop Contributions To Other Tax-Deferred Accounts?

Many people wonder if they should stop all contributions to other tax-deferred accounts to build their savings funds. If you were didn't contribute $19,000 to your 401(k), for example, then you could put that money towards an emergency fund.

Whether or not you should do this is highly personal, and there isn't a one-size-fits-all answer. For example, if your employer has a very generous 401(k) match, it wouldn't make much sense to stop receiving that free matching money. Similarly, if you anticipate significant medical expenses, not contributing to your HSA might be problematic since then those expenses will likely come out of your emergency fund anyways.

The best approach is usually a moderated one. If your employer matches your 401(k) contributions up to 6% of your salary, contribute just enough into your 401(k) to receive that match, and the rest can go towards building your emergency fund. Similarly, if you do not expect major medical bills, perhaps you reduce your contributions to your HSA temporarily while you are creating an emergency fund. Then once you have at least the short-term fund built, maybe then you resume the contributions. The key is not to become so obsessed with retirement savings that you lose sight of the need for emergency savings.

Build Your Emergency Fund Now

Unforeseen expenses can happen at any time. You want to make sure that you are ready so you don't find yourself struggling to come up with the money to pay for them. If you haven't already done so, start building both a short-term and long-term emergency fund to pay for one month and one year's worth of expenses, respectively. Remember that while retirement is essential, you also need money for your day-to-day life!

Cash Value Life Insurance: Thinking Like A Bank

Life insurance policies can be somewhat complicated. There are a lot of "moving parts" to a plan that can make it difficult to understand. There's the base premium that you pay, but then there's also a cash value of the policy. You can take loans against that cash value or even withdraw it. There are riders and additions you can add to modify the plan and make it different than the "stock" offering. In short, it can be not very clear.

However, life insurance plans are also a powerful way for high-income individuals to create and preserve wealth. One of those life insurance policy types is called the permanent cash value plan. It maximizes the amount of cash you have available immediately while still providing significant benefits.

What Is A Permanent Cash Value Life Insurance Policy?

The best way to analyze this plan type is to look at each word to understand its meaning.

There are two types of life insurance. Term policies mature after a certain number of years. For example, you might buy a policy that expires after 20 or 30 years. Permanent life insurance policies are valid for as long as you are alive.

They never expire, and you never stop contributing to them. They are active for as long as you live.

A cash value policy has a portion that is available as cash. You can use the cash portion as a source for loans, for withdrawals, or you can even use it to pay policy premiums. The cash value is a portion of the policy with which you can do whatever you want. It's effectively like a savings account.

Therefore, these policies are ones that never expire and that have a portion that you can access as cash.

Thinking Like A Bank: Buying High Cash Value Plans

Some high net worth individuals use high permanent cash value plans to create a bank. The idea is that you can create a massive tax-deferred fund that offers quite a bit of flexibility with loans and other withdrawals. However, setting this up requires a bit of legwork.

A high cash value policy is one that has a very minimal death benefit and a maximum cash value. Think along the lines of $25,000 as a death benefit and many hundreds of thousands in cash value. You'll want a life insurance policy that is permanent, with a paid-up additions rider.

Paid-up additions (PUAs) are contributions made above the required premiums that immediately contribute to both the death benefit and cash value of the policy. These paid-up additions generate dividends, which you can then use to purchase additional paid-up additions. The paid-up additions rider stipulates that you can buy these PUAs at any time without needing evidence of insurability. Your goal is to increase the cash value of your plan, and PUAs plus the rider allow you to do that.

The money that is in your cash value portion grows tax-free. You pay taxes on the money you contribute to your cash value portion, but the amount you earn while the money is in the policy is not subject to tax. Typically, the earnings rate within the life insurance policy is better than you can get in savings accounts, CDs, or bonds. Additionally, the earnings rate is usually guaranteed. Since you're not subject to tax, the money in the account can keep compounding.

Your Life Insurance Funds Your Retirement Dreams

To withdraw money out of your cash value portion of the life insurance policy, you have two primary options. First, you can cash out the cash surrender value (this is usually not the best option since it triggers taxation). Second, you can borrow against that value. Many people hear the word "borrow" and think this is a bad thing. In this particular case, it's a good thing.

Many people believe that these life insurance loans are like 401(k) loans. With a 401(k), your plan provider sells your equities, and you pay yourself back with interest. While you have lent yourself the money, you lose out on whatever income those equities would have produced. You'll have no dividends or capital appreciation.

With a life insurance loan, you're not borrowing against yourself. The money typically comes out of the life insurance company's general fund. That leaves your cash sitting in the cash value portion happily accruing the benefits of compound interest while you enjoy it.

How does this work in practice? Consider the following example. Suppose you have $500,000 in the cash value portion of your life insurance policy. You take out a loan for $25,000 to cover some expenses. Since it's your money, there are no stringent repayment requirements. You can make interest-only payments. You can pay nothing. You can wait until the death benefit portion of the policy pays off the loan. It's up to you. However, even with this $25,000 loaned out, your policy still sits at $500,000. In one year it earns 5% or $25,000. The cash balance is $525,000.

You take another $25,000 loan out. Now you have $50,000 borrowed. The cash value earns another 5% and sits at $551,250. Your cash value is greater than the sum of money you have borrowed. Your policy is gaining on the full amount tax-deferred, while your loan is only accruing interest on what you owe.

In effect, you become a bank for yourself. You have a pool of money that continues to earn money from which you can take loans or withdrawals. It offers a tremendous amount of flexibility. The best part about it is that when you pass away, your death benefit can clean up any unpaid fees, interest, etc., leaving the entire cash value to your loved ones. It's a bit of a creative idea to defer taxation, but it works!

Tax-Deferred Growth With A Permanent Cash Value Life Insurance Policy

If you are looking for tax-deferred growth, you may wish to consider a permanent cash value policy for life insurance. The name is a little misleading since the purpose of the plan isn't life insurance, but rather to take advantage of tax rules that allow for tax-deferred growth for cash portions of the policy. By using these regulations advantageously, you can effectively be a bank and lend yourself money. You'll create lots of cash flow and be able to have your investments grow while simultaneously borrowing money to fund your retirement dreams and goals. If you think a high cash value plan might work for you, speak with a financial advisor today.

HSA Accounts: Triple Tax Savings

The HSA (health spending account) is an account designed to allow people with high deductible health care plans to pay for medical expenses using pre-tax dollars. People contribute to these plans via a pre-tax deduction from their paychecks. There are no income restrictions with HSAs. As long as you have a high deductible health plan, you can have a health spending account.

HSAs are famous for their "triple tax savings." If used right, you avoid income tax on contributions, investment growth, and withdrawals. In this post, we'll explore HSAs more in-depth and take a look at how those tax savings play an essential part in your overall retirement strategy. Whether you are looking to retire at 65 or you're opting for the FIRE idea (Financially Independent Retire Early), having the HSA set up will likely be a critical aspect of achieving that goal.

What Are Health Savings Accounts

Health Savings Accounts are relatively new. George Bush enacted a bill in 2003 called the "Medicare Prescription Drug, Improvement, and Modernization Act," which created the Health Savings Account. The primary purpose of this bill was not to construct the HSA, but rather to improve Medicare offerings concerning prescription drugs.

In practice, these accounts work very much like individual retirement accounts (IRAs) with a few key differences.

First, unlike IRAs, you must be covered by a high-deductible health plan to have an HSA. As defined by the IRS, a high-deductible plan is one that has higher than average deductibles for medical expenses. Currently, the IRS defines this range as $1,350 to $6,650 for single persons or $2,700 to $13,300 for families [1]. If you have a health plan with deductibles in those ranges, then you qualify for an HSA. There are a couple of other qualification rules as well, but for most high-income earners during their careers, these extra qualifications will not apply.

Second, an HSA has different contribution limits than an IRA. For single people, the limit is $3,500 (which is $2,500 less than an IRA). However, for families, that amount doubles to $7,000, which is more than the $6,000 limit in 2019 for an IRA.

Finally, unlike IRAs, you can withdraw the contributions to your HSA tax-free if you use those contributions for qualified medical expenses. As with most tax-related laws, the rules of what qualifies are nuanced, but most costs you would expect are eligible. Going to the doctor, sitting in the ER, and buying prescription drugs can all be reimbursed with tax-free HSA money.

Other than that, the account types function very similarly. They're both self-directed. You can pick investments to help the funds grow, or you can leave the money in there like a bank account. You don't pay tax on the contributions to the HSA, and you don't pay taxes on any of the income or capital gains that money earns while the funds are still in the HSA. When you withdraw, you also don't pay any tax on that money if you use it for a qualified medical expense. If you withdraw money for a non-qualified expense before 65, you pay a 20% penalty. If you withdraw after 65, the additional 20% no longer applies, but you will still have to pay your standard income tax rate.

Since you deposit the money tax-free, the funds grow tax-free, and you do not need to pay taxes on the money if used for qualifying medical expenses, the HSA has triple tax savings. The health spending account is unique in this regard, and that is what makes it so crucial for high-income earners.

Using The HSA As A Supplemental Retirement Vehicle

The unique properties of an HSA make it attractive for high-income earners as part of a comprehensive retirement strategy. At first glance, it's obvious how this account benefits. If your effective tax rate is 40%, for example, then any money you put in the HSA and use for medical expenses automatically saves you from paying that elevated tax rate. That alone should be enough to encourage high-income earners to explore HSAs.

However, there are some nuanced benefits, as well. You do not need to reimburse yourself for expenses at the same time you incur those charges. As long as the HSA was active at the same time the cost happened, you can withdraw the funds in the future at any time. This nuance means that you can pay for your expenses out-of-pocket now, keep the receipt, and then when you retire, you can still withdraw that money tax-free. In the meantime, though, the money in the HSA can continue to grow unencumbered.

As a quick example, let's suppose you have $30,000 in your HSA. You have a year in which you incur $10,000 in medical expenses. You could withdraw that money immediately, or you can leave it in your HSA. If you incurred those expenses when you were 30 and chose to withdraw that money, at a 5% return, the future value of that $20,000 at age 55 would be $67,727.10. However, if you elect to defer requesting reimbursement, the future value would be $101,590.65. At age 55, you could still claim the original $10,000 through tax-free. However, now you have $91,590.65 to pay for medical costs during retirement instead of $67,727.10.

Additionally, HSAs do not have a required distribution timeframe. You are free to request withdrawals at any age, and there are no minimum distribution amounts. Therefore, you can let HSA funds continue to grow for as long as you want and only take withdrawals when necessary during retirement. You can exhaust other accounts, like your 401(k) or IRA first, before touching your HSA funds.

Take Advantage Of The HSAs Triple Tax Savings

The triple tax savings make the HSA an essential account for a comprehensive retirement strategy. It complements other retirement accounts like the 401(k) and the IRA by providing tax-free contributions, earnings, and withdrawals for qualified medical expenses. The fact that it works much like an IRA after age 65 makes it very useful for retirement savings as well.

If your employer offers a high-deductible health plan, consider taking it and having an HSA as well. Putting money in there will help you during retirement, whether that's early retirement or one at a more traditional age!

Tax Deferred Accounts

To encourage savings, Congress has provisioned many tax-sheltered savings accounts. Although there are nuances with each account, the premise is simple: you do not pay any taxes on your contributions or the investments' growth. When it comes time to withdraw, however, you must pay regular income tax on those withdrawals. Each account type has defined contribution limits and also typically has an age by which you must start withdrawing money. This age is 59.5, in most cases.

The benefit to high-income earners is that the money contributed avoids the top tax rate. If you are making $250,000 per year, then all money above $204,000 is taxed at 35% federally. If you put $20,000 per year into these accounts, you would save at least $7,000 in taxes. That money would then continue to grow, tax-free, until retirement. At that point, assuming you withdraw less in your retirement years, that original contribution would be taxed at the 12% rate.

There are five top tax-deferred savings accounts that you should know about: IRA, 401(k), Simple IRA/401(k), SEP IRA, and 403(b). Not all accounts will apply for all individuals, but if you have a substantial income, it's in your best interest to contribute to as many of these accounts as you can!

Traditional IRA: Simple and Easy

The traditional IRA is the most straightforward tax-deferred account you can open. Most banks and credit unions offer an IRA. It works exactly like a standard bank or brokerage account. You can make contributions and invest the money how you see fit. If the IRA is a standard bank account, it will earn interest. If it's a brokerage, you can invest in any US equities you want. You can even trade Forex in it if you wish. It's 100% in your control. There's no limit on the number of accounts you can have either - having multiple IRAs is entirely permissible.

Annually, you can contribute up to $6,000 per year to all the IRAs you have. The contribution limit remains fixed, so even if you have multiple accounts, you can only contribute up to $6,000 amongst all of them. If you are 50 or older, that limit rises to $7,000.

Contributions go on your 1040, and your contributions reduce your income. Since your income is lower, you pay less in tax. There is no way to have an employer directly contribute to an IRA. You must first add after-tax dollars and then have the income tax you paid "reimbursed" when you file next April. These transfers do not reduce your social security or Medicare obligations.

You can withdraw the money after age 59.5 and only pay income tax. Before 59, all withdrawals are subject to a 10% penalty on top of the standard income taxes.

Traditional 401(k): The Account Type That Defers The Most In Tax

The 401(k) is, by far, the most popular way to save for retirement. Congress added the section in the Internal Revenue Code for these savings vehicles back in 1978. Today, 65% of all workers have access to a 401(k) savings plan through work. Most, if not all, large corporations provide this plan for their employees.

Conceptually, the traditional 401(k) is similar to an IRA. You contribute pre-tax dollars, and the money compounds without taxation in the account. At age 59.5, you can begin withdrawing your money. You will have to pay income tax on it, but you won't be subject to the 10% penalty at that time. Before 59.5, much like an IRA, the 10% penalty applies.

However, a 401(k) is different in significant ways. The contribution limit is much higher. You can contribute $19,000 per year pre-tax to your 401(k). Some employers offer a matching contribution. That match doesn't count against your limit. Therefore, if you had an employer match $0.50 to every $1 you contribute, you could contribute $19,000, and they could put in $9,500 for a massive $28,500 total in tax-deferred savings per year.

Since the employer offers the plan, they have much more control. They can restrict the account only to allow certain investments. Unless you have a qualifying hardship, you cannot withdraw the money in your 401(k) if you are still working for that employer. You can, however, take a loan against your 401(k) up to $50,000 for a maximum term of 5 years (or 15 years if you are using the money to buy a principal residence).

If your employer offers a 401(k), contribute to it now. It's a great way to save for retirement.

SIMPLE IRA and SIMPLE 401(k): Retirement Savings For Small Businesses

Businesses with fewer than 100 employees can establish an IRA and 401(k) for their employees with minimal paperwork. These SIMPLE (Savings Incentive Match Plan for Employees of Small Employers) plans help small businesses encourage employees to save for retirement.

Despite sharing the same names as the traditional variants, there are many key differences. SIMPLE IRAs have a maximum contribution limit of $13,000, and employees make those contributions via salary withholding (much like traditional 401(k)s). Employers must contribute to these plans. They either pitch in 2% for every employee or match 3% of all contributions dollar-for-dollar.

SIMPLE 401(k)s have the same contribution limits and matching requirements. The difference is that, much like traditional 401(k)s, they offer hardship withdrawals and loan options. Employers have to file more paperwork to provide a 401(k) for their employees.

SEP IRA: Small Business Owners Should Have This

A Simplified Employee Pension (SEP) IRA is an investment vehicle for small-business owners. These are not vehicles in which employees contribute a portion of their salary. Instead, the SEP IRA enables profit sharing. Owners can elect to pay up to 25% of their and their employees' wages to each SEP IRA. The maximum contribution is $56,000. All owners and employees must receive the same percentage.

One interesting fact about the SEP IRA is that it "stacks" with other investment vehicles. So if you were working for a company and had a side business with a SEP IRA, you could, in theory, save

- $7,000 via a traditional IRA
- $19,000 + matching contributions via a traditional 401(k)
- $56,000 via your business SEP IRA

The total tax-deferred savings, in this case, would be $86,000. Some people elect to hold investments and real estate rental properties in a company to have a SEP IRA. Check your MAGI (Modified Adjusted Gross Income) and AGI for what deductions will be available to you.

Like all the other account types, the withdrawal age is at 59.5, and you must pay a 10% penalty on withdrawals before that age.

403(b): Much Like A 401(k) But For Public Schools and Tax Exempt Orgs

A 403(b) is essentially a 401(k) but for public schools and other tax-exempt organizations. This plan offers the same contribution limits as a 401(k) and has the same penalties and withdrawal age. Typically the financial institutions that administer 403(b) plans offer investments tailored to the public sector. These can have lower expense ratios.

One small difference between a 401(k) and 403(b) is the ability to make catch up contributions. If you have been working for the same employer for 15 years and your average annual deposit was less than $5,000, then you can contribute $3,000 per year extra up to a maximum of $15,000. This additional room helps people who may be making quite a bit later in their career make up for not contributing as much earlier.

Choosing The Right Retirement Vehicles

Planning for retirement is critical. If you are a high-income earner, there are many ways to defer taxes and save for retirement. The most popular are the traditional IRA and either the SIMPLE IRA or traditional 401(k). If you have rental properties or a side business, you may wish to consider forming a SEP IRA to reduce your tax liability on that income further. If your primary source of income is from that business, then having a SEP IRA is a great way to defer taxation on a substantial amount of money.

Deferring taxes is a fantastic way to maximize your savings for retirement. Each of these vehicles lets you pay Uncle Sam less money now and less money later on in life! Consider opening any applicable tax-deferred account today to reduce your tax bill for the year.

Roth IRAs And 401(k)s

When people think of IRAs and 401(k)s, they typically think of traditional ones. They envision accounts in which you make pre-tax contributions, and the money continues to grow without taxation. Then, when it comes time to withdraw the money, it is taxed at regular income rates. These are traditional IRAs and 401(k)s, and many people have them.

Less known, however, are Roth IRAs and 401(k)s. These accounts function differently than their traditional counterparts. With these accounts, you contribute after-tax dollars. The money grows tax-free while in there. Then, when you withdraw the money, it is not taxed. It's a little like the opposite of the traditional version - instead of avoiding taxes now but paying them later, a Roth IRA or 401(k) lets you pay them now, but prevent them when you reach 59.5.

In this section, we'll take a look at these two investment types. We'll explore the history and also examine why people might choose a Roth IRA or 401(k) as opposed to a traditional one.

The History of Roth

The Roth IRA is a relatively new invention. Lawmakers codified the traditional 401(k) back in 1978. The Roth IRA didn't exist until 1997. Lawmakers added it as part of the Taxpayer Relief Act, and it was signed into law by

President Bill Clinton. The account's name comes from one of the bill's sponsors, William Roth of Delaware.

Since this account type is only 20 years old, many people who have been in the workforce for many years may not be aware of it. While the traditional IRA and 401(k) is the most popular retirement saving option, the Roth versions have notable positives that make it worth considering.

Income Limits

One caveat to the Roth IRA and 401(k) is that both account types are subject to income limits. If you are married and filing a joint return, then you can contribute the maximum if you earn less than $193,000 per year. You can add a partial amount to your account if you earn between $193,000 and $203,000 per year. For those making more than $203,000 combined income, only the traditional IRA and 401(k) options are allowed.

Single filers can contribute the full amount up to $122,000 and can add money to the account partially between $122,000 and $137,000. Non-married people making over $137,000 cannot use a Roth account.

Contribution Limits

The contribution limits on Roth IRAs and 401(k)s are the same as their traditional variants. For IRAs, the limit is $6,000. For a Roth 401(k), the limit is $19,000 annually.

If you are over 50, those limits rise to $7,000 and $25,000, respectively.

It's worth keeping in mind that those contribution limits are in after-tax dollars. Many people correctly point out that a Roth IRA has a "higher" contribution limit in that $6,000 after-tax would be the equivalent of $9,230 pre-tax dollars, if the government would have taxed that money at the rate of 35%.

Like traditional 401(k)s, Roth accounts allow for matching contributions. If your employer offers a 3% match or something similar, you won't lose that if you elect for a Roth 401(k).

How These Plans Work

Conceptually, the Roth versions of these plans function similarly to the traditional ones. You contribute money to them, and the funds are free to grow without taxation. Pre-tax payroll income reductions are the way to fund a traditional 401(k). Post-tax payroll deductions are the way to contribute to a Roth 401(k).

The difference, therefore, is when you pay tax. A traditional 401(k) defers the income tax right now, but you pay it when you take out the money during retirement. A Roth 401(k) has you paying the income tax now, but when you want to withdraw, it's 100% yours.

Depending on your retirement plans, the difference between the two can be extraordinary. Consider the following scenario. Suppose someone has $10,000 worth of pre-tax funds to contribute to their IRA. Further, suppose the tax rate for that money is 30%.

That person could contribute $10,000 to a traditional IRA or $7,000 to a Roth one ($10,000 - $3,000 in taxes).

If the rate of return is 5% per year for 30 years, the traditional IRA option would be worth $43,219. The Roth IRA option would be worth $30,254. Remember, though, that the $43k is not all yours. You'll still need to pay tax on it. If your effective tax rate is 30%, the Roth and traditional IRAs break even. Above that, and the Roth was more advantageous. Below that and the traditional IRA was better.

It's no coincidence that the 30% breakeven rate is the same as the original tax rate. Roth IRAs are more beneficial if you expect your tax rate to increase during retirement. If you expect your tax rate to decrease, then the traditional IRA is typically the way to go.

Withdrawal Rules

There are a couple of differences in withdrawal rules that make Roth IRAs attractive if you think you may want to have access to the funds penalty-free at some point.

Much like traditional IRAs, Roth ones allow for penalty-free withdrawals at age 59.5. However, since you have already paid taxes on your Roth contributions, you can withdraw those at any time tax and penalty-free. You only pay penalties and income tax on the earnings portion.

If you have a Roth account worth $1,100 ($1,000 contributions, $100 earnings), then you can withdraw up to $1,000 with no penalties or taxes. In that respect, Roth accounts have an edge. If you don't need the money, you can treat it like a tax-free savings account. If you do need the money, then you can at least avoid paying the 10% penalty on a portion of the funds.

Roth IRAs and 401(k)s Summary

If you are below the income limits, take a look at Roth accounts. Often it makes sense to go with a traditional IRA, but if you expect your tax rate to increase during retirement, then the Roth accounts probably make the most sense. One combination that high-income people may wish to consider is a traditional 401(k) with a Roth IRA. The 401(k) lets you defer taxation on the bulk of your retirement savings, while the Roth enables you to save money for your retirement in a liquid way. If you need the cash, you can always withdraw the sum of the contributions without paying penalties.

Backdoor Roth IRAs: Roth Accounts At Any Income Level

Many highly compensated employees are familiar with the income limits on a Roth IRA. If your adjusted gross income exceeds $122,000 for a single filer or $193,000 for a married taxpayer, you cannot contribute to a Roth IRA. These income limits do not apply for a traditional IRA, however. The Roth IRA takes after-tax contributions. Any gains made with that after-tax money have no taxes upon withdrawal. With a traditional IRA, contributions are tax-deductible. Once you take the money out, that withdrawal is subject to ordinary income tax.

There is an entirely legitimate way to bypass this restriction on Roth IRAs. If you are earning more than the maximum Roth income limits, read on to learn how to obtain a Roth IRA and when it makes sense to do so.

Converting From Traditional to Roth

The US tax code permits converting from a traditional IRA to a Roth IRA. There are no income restrictions on this conversion. This technicality means that you can open a traditional IRA, make the contributions to it, and then convert it to a Roth IRA. This simple conversion effectively bypasses the income restrictions that are in place for contributions to a Roth IRA.

The process for doing this is relatively straightforward. The IRS outlines three ways to achieve this goal:

- Obtain a check withdrawal for the funds in the traditional IRA and deposit them into a Roth IRA within 60 days.
- Transfer the funds from a traditional account to the Roth one at another institution (much like a rollover).
- Transfer the funds between the two account types at the same financial institution.

At the time of conversion, you are responsible for any taxes owed on the traditional IRA money. It is like you withdrew it all, paid tax on it (but no penalties), and then deposited that after-tax money into a Roth account. If you are converting a $100,000 traditional account to Roth, that will be a hefty tax bill. If you are saving your yearly $6,000 contribution every year, then the only taxes you need to pay are the ones you would have paid anyway had you put it in a Roth account. You won't pay any extra income taxes for this conversion.

It is worth noting that you needn't convert from a new traditional IRA to a new Roth IRA. You can convert existing funds from a traditional IRA that you already have and place those in a Roth IRA you also already have. However, you must pay tax on any money that you convert (contributions and earnings). There is also a five year waiting period for withdrawing those funds after the conversion. So you cannot convert from a traditional IRA to a Roth one and initiate a penalty-free withdrawal immediately. You would need to wait five years to access that money.

When Does This Conversion Make Sense?

If you are making at least the minimum income to be ineligible for a Roth IRA, you are paying at least 24% in taxes on that money. The money you would be contributing to your Roth would is taxable at one of the top four rates. Due to this, generally, it is advisable to defer taxes so you will pay less once you withdraw the money.

However, there are some circumstances in which taking advantage of this backdoor Roth conversion makes sense. These circumstances certainly do not apply to everyone, but they will for some highly compensated individuals.

For high net worth individuals, Roth IRAs offer the most flexibility in terms of distribution. Traditional IRAs have required minimum distributions that start at age 70 1/2. Roth IRAs have no such requirement. If you want to let this money grow tax-free for the longest, then the best way to achieve that is through a Roth IRA. Both IRAs offer penalty-free withdrawals starting at age 59 1/2.

If you expect that your retirement tax bracket will be higher than your current one (either you will have more income, or you believe tax rates will continue to rise), then paying the tax liability now makes sense. Most people should see their retirement income taxes decrease. However, there are some circumstances in which that might not be true. You might know that you will be receiving an inheritance or have a business that will be providing substantial income during retirement. If that's the case, then it's reasonable to assume your tax brackets will rise instead of fall.

Finally, if you want the most flexibility with your money, the Roth IRA is the way to achieve that. A Roth IRA works much like a traditional savings account. As long as you only withdraw what you have contributed, there are no taxes and no penalties. Many people like to have a savings fund in their Roth IRA that grows tax-free, but if they need the money, they know they can take out their contributions at least without incurring a penalty.

Roth IRAs As Savings Vehicles For Retirement

Roth IRAs tend to be less preferred for retirement savings than traditional ones because you need to pay income tax upfront as opposed to deferring it for later. On the flip side, it's nice to be able to withdraw tax-free money during retirement. There's also a "mental simplicity" related to Roth IRAs: it's nice to know that what is in the accounts is yours. There will be no income tax on it so that $100,000 isn't $100k minus 20% in income tax. It's $100k that is yours to use.

Converting a traditional IRA to a Roth IRA is relatively easy to do. The financial institution with whom you have the account will be well-versed in how to do this. All you need to do is contact them, and they can start the process for you. If your traditional IRA has contributions from other years, you will need to pay tax on those contributions. You do not need to convert the entire account, however. You can elect to have a portion of your account converted each year to minimize the tax liability.

College 529 Plan Savings

Education is incredibly pricey. The cost of a college degree has risen dramatically within the past 20 years. For private universities, tuition rose 154% in that time frame. Out-of-state tuition at public universities rose 181% while in-state tuition has gone up the most at 221%. Within 20 years, college costs have nearly tripled in the United States. Experts do not expect that trend to slow down. If anything, as the domestic and international demand for US education becomes greater, college costs will likely continue to skyrocket.

If you are a parent, you know how much you want to be able to provide the best possible education for your children. Ensuring they can focus on their studies and not have to sweat finances is a fantastic way to help them through school and on to a successful career. Many parents know that the 529 plan is the way to save for school. However, it's not just useful for dependents. The 529 plan is significantly more flexible. If you or anyone in your immediate family will want to go to school in the future, opening a 529 is essential to making that dream a reality.

The 529's History

Despite 529 plans being available nationwide, the origin of the idea did not come at the federal level. The original idea came from Michigan. With college costs rising in the state, legislators created the Michigan Education Trust. This state program allowed residents to pay a fixed fee for college now, and the trust would pay the full amount of tuition to one of the universities in Michigan when the resident was ready to attend.

After some back and forth with the courts and the IRS, Congress decided to intervene and make college savings plans part of the Internal Revenue Code. The section that spells out the rules of these plans is 529, hence the name. Those changes became officially part of the law as part of the Taxpayer Relief Act of 1997 under President Bill Clinton.

Tax-Deferred College Savings

The primary purpose of the 529 is to save for higher education expenses. Money contributed to this plan is all post-tax. There are no upfront tax savings with contributions. However, once in the program, your funds can grow without taxation. When you withdraw, so long as you use the money for qualified education expenses, the money you take out is tax-free. Any capital gains, dividends, and other income earned while the money was in the 529 has zero income tax.

If you don't use the money for qualified education expenses, then any amount over what you have contributed (i.e., any capital gains, etc.) is subject to regular income tax, and you will also have to pay a 10%

penalty. If your state allowed income tax deductions on 529 contributions, then you would also have to pay those back.

What Expenses Qualify?

As you might expect, standard higher education expenses qualify. College tuition counts. Vocational and trade school expenses count. You can also use these funds to pay for fees associated with college as well (like access fees, library fees, etc.).

Many parents don't realize that there are many additional eligible expenses. Room and board is a qualified expense if paid directly to the university. Food and meal plans, books, and computers can all be qualified expenses.

Parents should also be aware that these qualified expenses needn't be at the college level. Elementary and secondary school expenses are also qualified. If you know that your child will be attending a private primary or secondary school, you can set up a 529 for them to help save for those expenses early. Some of these schools are not cheap, and having a tax-sheltered way to pay for those costs is immensely helpful.

Who Can Use This Plan?

While the original intent of the 529 was for parents to save for education expenses for children, the reality is that any family member can be the beneficiary of a 529 plan, including yourself. You can also change beneficiaries without any penalties so long as it is another family member. The IRS defines that term broadly so parents, children, step-children, spouses, and siblings all count.

Therefore, you can avoid the 10% penalty by transferring to another family member. Suppose you saved $200,000 in a 529 plan with your child as beneficiary. Let's say they decide to go to a state school that only costs $100,000. You'll have $100,000 left. You can then change the beneficiary on that plan to be yourself, your spouse, or another one of your children. They can withdraw that money tax-free to pay for their education costs. Maybe you've always wanted a Ph.D., or maybe your spouse wants to get a Masters. Either way, the money you save can be put to use.

A Note On Scholarships

If the beneficiary of the 529 plan obtains a scholarship that reduces the cost of their tuition, you can withdraw that amount of gains and not pay any penalty (but you will pay income tax). Suppose your child goes to school on a full scholarship. You then withdraw all the money in the 529. You will have to pay ordinary income tax on the gains within the plan. However, you will not need to pay the 10% penalty on anything. Therefore, saving in the 529 plan is still beneficial even if your child can go to school for free.

Start Saving For Education Today

Private elementary and secondary schools are expensive. College costs are expected to continue to rise in the coming decades. In short, education is incredibly pricey, and the expenses related to schooling are showing no signs of slowing down. A 529 plan lets you save after-tax money for these expenses. Any amount you earn has no taxes when you use it for qualified education expenses.

The 529 plan is incredibly flexible in terms of beneficiaries and qualified expenses. Open one up sooner rather than later so you can ensure you and your loved ones have the money they need to further their educational aspirations.

Mega Backdoor Roth Accounts

Highly compensated employees may have heard the term "mega backdoor Roth" before. The name sounds justifiably impressive. It allows you to save up to $37,000 in a Roth IRA or Roth 401(k). If you do that for 30 years, assuming a 5% return on investment, you will have approximately $2.5 million that you can withdraw, tax-free. Providing that money continues to earn 5% even after you retire, that $2.5 million in cash would produce $125,000 in yearly tax-free income for you to use.

For most people, doing a mega backdoor Roth allows them to have true worry-free financial independence during retirement. It's a substantial amount of tax-free money to have saved. The steps to accomplish this are a little complex, and not all employees can take advantage of this. Let's take a look at what you need to achieve this fantastic savings feat and what steps you would need to take.

Who Can Do A Mega Backdoor Roth?

There are some prerequisites to be able to take advantage of the mega backdoor Roth. The first, and perhaps most obvious one, is that if you cannot already max out your 401(k) contributions of $19,000 per year and your IRA contributions of $6,000, then the mega backdoor Roth doesn't apply. The mega backdoor is so that you can save above those limits. Even if you aren't presently maxing those out, knowing about this backdoor is useful for when you are contributing the maximum amounts.

Second, your employer must have a 401(k) plan that supports a couple of features. It must allow for in-service withdrawals (some 401(k)s do not permit general in-service withdrawals, but they will permit withdrawals for this particular scenario). The plan must also allow for after-tax contributions above the $19,000 pre-tax limit.

Check with your 401(k) plan administrator to see if your plan has all these prerequisites. If it does, and you can contribute more than $25,000 per year (the pre-tax limits), then you can take advantage of the mega backdoor Roth.

A Little Known Property of 401(k)s

Most people believe that the maximum contribution to a 401(k) is $19,000. While this is mostly true, it doesn't tell the whole story. The maximum amount that an employee may contribute to a 401(k) is $19,000. The maximum total contribution to a 401(k) from any source (employee, employer, after-tax, etc.) is $56,000. If the IRS didn't set a limit like this, then an employer could, in theory, pay an employee's $500k salary with $250k in cash and $250k tax-deferred in their 401(k). With this restriction in place, employers and employees can only get so creative when deferring taxes.

The Mega Backdoor Roth Emerges

This little-known fact is what allows the mega backdoor Roth to happen. You will be contributing the maximum in pre-tax money. That's $19,000 which leaves $37,000 left. If your employer matches any of your 401(k) contributions, that also counts against the $56,000 limit. Assume that your employer kicks in $6,000 per year. Now you are left with $31,000.

You can contribute that $31k as after-tax money to your 401(k). Then, you can request a rollover of that money immediately into a Roth IRA. Voila! You now have $31,000 in savings that will be entirely tax-free once you withdraw during your retirement.

Your plan must permit after-tax contributions, and typically you will need to contact your provider to create a new after-tax account. This account will be with your employer's 401(k) provider but won't be the same bucket of money as your pre-tax or Roth contributions. If you do not use the funds in this account as part of the mega backdoor Roth scheme, it grows tax-free, but you will have to pay taxes on all earnings upon distribution.

Steps To Execute The Mega Backdoor Roth Scheme

There are three main steps to completing the mega backdoor Roth scheme.

1. Maximize your pre-tax 401(k) contributions. You should get as much of a match as your employer will allow.

2. Maximize your after-tax 401(k) contributions. Note that these are not Roth contributions. There will be an option with your employer to explicitly request "after-tax" contributions. You want to maximize that.

3. Withdraw the after-tax portion to a Roth IRA. If your 401(k) allows for in-service withdrawals, you can request a rollover to a Roth IRA. If you have any earnings, then you will owe tax on those earnings. However, if you ask for the withdrawal reasonably quickly, those earnings should be minimal.

After making the withdrawal, your Roth IRA will now have that money, and any income it produces will be completely tax-free. Some 401(k)s have what is called an "In-Plan Roth Conversion." This term is effectively a rollover to a Roth IRA. It's just a different way of doing it behind-the-scenes. As far as your concerned, whether you make a withdrawal for an in-plan conversion, the money winds up in your Roth IRA.

The Mega Backdoor Roth Makes The 401(k) A True Savings Vehicle

The mega backdoor Roth makes the 401(k) shine as a savings vehicle for well-paid employees. It also works great for entrepreneurs who can have complete control over their 401(k)s and what the plans allow. To be able to save $56,000 in combined pre-tax employee dollars, pre-tax employer money, and Roth dollars is substantial. By using the mega backdoor Roth in conjunction with other savings vehicles, like HSAs, you can be putting away upwards of $60,000 with some form of tax-sheltering.

At even a 5% rate of return, this could result in a $4 million nest egg of combined pre and post-tax money. Having that combination is also critical in retirement. You can withdraw pre-tax funds in the lower tax brackets. To supplement that income, you can then withdraw Roth funds. By doing this, you can ensure that you keep your tax rate low on the pre-tax money, which maximizes your tax savings.

Check With Your Employer's Plan

If you find yourself in a position where you could take advantage of the mega backdoor Roth, you should check with your employer's plan. There is no downside to making these contributions if your 401(k) plan lets you. It's a great way to have tens of thousands of dollars growing tax-free for your retirement. The mega backdoor also makes the 401(k) a much better savings platform for highly-compensated employees. The standard 401(k) limit of $19,000 doesn't allow for too much in terms of saving, but with the mega backdoor option, saving $56,000 every year for retirement is quite substantial. That amount alone, assuming you can contribute for 30 years or so, has the potential to fund your retirement goals.

Non-Qualified Deferred Compensation Plans

Many high-income individuals know about 401(k)s and IRAs. These plans are "qualified" tax-deferred plans. The term "qualified" means that the retirement account meets the standards of the Employee Retirement Income Security Act. This act ensures transparency and protects workers' income. The reason that 401(k)s and IRAs are so popular and so well-known is that they are easy for employers to set up and have robust protections for employees. They also allow employees to defer taxes on some of their income.

However, even if you max out your 401(k) and IRA, you're still looking at deferring taxes on a maximum amount of $32,000 per year (if you are over 55 and making catch-up contributions). For executives and other high six-figure or even seven-figure employees, that represents a small percentage of their annual income. Much of their income will be subject to an income tax rate that exceeds 30%.

To get around these restrictions, companies frequently offer key employees some form of a nonqualified deferred compensation plan. These plans aim to shelter income from taxation above and beyond the standard limits of a 401(k) or IRA. Let's analyze what these plans are and how they can help high-income individuals minimize their tax bills during their working years.

What Is A Nonqualified Deferred Compensation Plan?

As you may have already guessed, a nonqualified plan is one that does not meet the standards of the ERISA (Employee Retirement Income Security Act). These plans are non-standard and are the result of negotiations between the employer and employee. A nonqualified deferred compensation plan is an agreement to defer some compensation until a future point in time. It is not an account, per se, but rather a contract between the company and employee.

Since it is not an account and not "qualified," a deferred compensation plan has no caps and fewer rules. A company can agree to defer compensation until an employee retires or an employee leaves the company. Or they can pick any other arbitrary date in the future.

Consider the following example. Suppose that John Doe earns $250,000 per year and makes approximately $250,000 per year extra in bonuses. His total compensation per year is $500,000. John maxes out his 401(k), his IRA, and his HSA. Between all of these, John can defer taxes on $28,500 of his income (assuming Mr. Doe is single and under 55 years of age). However, that represents just 5.7% of his annual salary and bonuses. If he maximizes his contributions every single year for 30 years, at a 5% return, John will have $2 million in retirement funds (pre-tax). While that's not too shabby, it's only 4x his current salary. Since these are pre-tax dollars, that means John will only be able to live for four years at his current lifestyle in retirement.

Let's consider a different scenario. Suppose the company at which John works says that they will put $100,000 of his bonuses per year in company stock until he retires. John accepts. He earns $250,000 in salary and $150,000 in additional monetary awards, which is plenty for living. The company agrees to have this money "earn" 5% each year, with an award date set 30 years in advance. John's pre-tax sum of accrued distributions is worth $9,000,000 in retirement. That's 18x his original $500,000 salary or 22.5x his revised $400,000 one.

By deferring just 20% extra of his income until retirement, John has significantly more saved and can retire with much more confidence. He's also saved quite a bit on taxes. That $100,000 would have been taxed at the top rate of 35% anyways. Now, when the company pays him out, he'll be taxed at much less.

Structure Of Nonqualified Plans

Due to the flexible nature of these arrangements, the IRS has some fairly strict regulations surrounding them. First, the plan must be in writing. No verbal agreements are allowed. Second, the written document must specify the amount to be paid, when the payment or payments will occur, and what event will trigger them. There are six permissible triggering events:

1. A fixed date, such as March 15, 2030;
2. Leaving the company (typically this is retirement);
3. Change in company ownership (such as a takeover);
4. Disability
5. Death
6. Emergency

The employee must also enter into this agreement the year before earning the compensation. You cannot have a great year and then elect to defer a portion of your salary.

The deferred amount also earns a reasonable rate of return, linked to some real asset (or options), an index, or a fixed percentage.

One Caveat

Unlike qualified plans, nonqualified ones may not have a physical account with real money in it that belongs to the employee. Instead, the "plan" is effectively nothing more than a written agreement between the employee and employer. Companies account for this plan as a liability on the balance sheet. There is no actual transfer of money that needs to take place.

Since there is no real account, these funds will pay creditors in the event of bankruptcy before paying you. Going back to the example in this article, if John Doe had been deferring $100,000 in compensation for 29 years and the company then went bankrupt, he could quickly lose a large portion of that deferred money.

Of course, if you are an executive that has five years to go until retirement, this is much less of a concern. If you are younger and want to defer compensation for 30 years, it's tough to predict which companies will still be successful. For example, in 1989, I doubt many people would have predicted the bankruptcy of Sears.

Nonqualified Plans Are Fantastic, If Used Correctly

If negotiated and written up correctly, nonqualified deferred compensation plans allow for significant tax-deferral opportunities. You can earn money at the top tax bracket and pay significantly less tax on that money in later years. Furthermore, these nonqualified plans are one of the only ways to bypass the fairly restrictive contribution limits of a standard HSA, IRA, and 401(k) trio. If you are a high-compensation employee and have access to a nonqualified deferred compensation plan, discuss the implications with your financial advisor. There's a good chance it makes sense to defer some of your income to a later date.

Why You Need A Regular Brokerage Account

It might seem strange to be discussing taxable accounts in a book that primarily focuses on tax-sheltered ones. After all, the discussion of tax-deferment is typically the focus of most financial planning articles. Who wants to pay tax when they don't need to? And aren't traditional taxable brokerage accounts precisely what these astute individuals are advising highly-compensated professionals to avoid?

While it is true that you should usually try and defer as much tax as possible, it's also true that tax-sheltered accounts frequently have significant restrictions. On a basic level, they all have some form of contribution limit. Whether you make $10,000 or $10 million per year, the maximum amount you can put in your 401(k) is $19,000 per year. For an employee making $500,000 per year, that amount represents less than 4% of their income. That's not much tax to be deferring.

The truth is, there will be times when you will need access to savings that are unencumbered by nuanced tax laws and regulations. In those situations, you need to have a regular, old-fashioned taxable brokerage account. Here are three key reasons why you need to have a conventional brokerage account in addition to tax-deferred ones.

Liquidity

Some employers don't allow for in-service 401(k) withdrawals. Suppose you're pinching every penny to maximize your contributions to your 401(k). You're going to feel pretty good about yourself! Then, one day, the water pipe bursts in your house and floods it. You need to replace the floors and repair the damage. Only the problem is that you have no savings. It all went to the 401(k), and you can't access that money while you're still working for the company. You might have $200k sitting in the 401(k), which would quickly pay for all your repairs, but you can't touch it without quitting.

Even if you were to withdraw it, you'd face steep IRS penalties for doing so. For a 401(k) the distribution penalty would be 10%. If you tried to pull the money out of your HSA, that percentage would rise to 20%. That's a steep price to pay for accessing your funds.

A regular taxable brokerage account doesn't have any of these issues. Since you paid tax on the money when it went in, and you pay income tax on anything you make, you can always withdraw that money to pay any bills that arise.

Put another way, saving in these tax-sheltered accounts is only useful if you can keep the money in there until retirement (or in the case of an HSA, until a qualified medical expense). If you don't have any liquid savings, then you'll invariably need access to some of those funds before retiring.

One important point to remember is that after-tax Roth contributions are not subject to a withdrawal penalty so long as the amount you withdraw is not over what you have put in over the years. Suppose you put $5,000 into a Roth IRA, and that grows to $10,000. If you withdraw the entire account, you would owe no tax or penalties on the first half, but you would owe taxes and a 10% penalty on the second half. Therefore, you can still have some liquidity with a Roth account, so long as you never withdraw more than you have put into it.

No Contribution Or Investment Limits

If you make $5 million per year, you can contribute every penny of your after-tax income to a regular brokerage account. There are no limits, and you don't have to worry about rules that eliminate your contribution room once you reach a certain income threshold. Put as much or as little in there as you want. The choice is yours!

Additionally, you can invest whatever you want in a regular account. If you feel the need to buy 500 shares of one company, you can do so. With a 401(k), investment choices are often reasonably limited. It is possible to have plans that allow stock trading, but those are somewhat rare. Usually, 401(k) plans have a pre-selected set of mutual funds from which you can choose.

There can also be an opportunity cost there as well. As a quick example, suppose there are indicators that the broader economy will slow down. If you contribute money to a 401(k), those funds will likely decrease. If you paid the tax on the cash, put it in a regular account, and shorted some stocks, maybe you'd gain some net worth. The opportunity cost is not super typical, but the limitation of the 401(k) investments can sometimes hinder people's ability to make the best use of that money.

No Mandatory Distributions

Tax-deferred plans have required minimum distribution dates. Of course, your brokerage account doesn't have these restrictions. If you want to leave the money in there until you are 90, you can do so. If you're going to withdraw them at 50, again, you can make that choice. The government will never force you to take money out of that account, and they'll never make you put money back into it. When you take it out and what you take it out for is 100% your choice.

Have Liquid Accounts And Tax-Sheltered Accounts

While it can be tempting, having your money reside only in tax-sheltered accounts is a recipe for disaster. Eventually, you will need access to some liquidity. Once you do, you'll wreak havoc on your financial situation, trying to access that money from those accounts (assuming you even can do so).

You need some liquidity. You need to have a conventional taxable brokerage account to go along with your 401(k), IRA, HSA, 529, SEP, or whatever other three-letter or number plans you have. That way, when things become tricky financially, you will have money from which you can draw. Using your 401(k) or another tax-deferred plan as your primary savings vehicle will likely cause problems down the road. Keep a brokerage account as well, so you don't need to dip into your retirement funds because a financial emergency happened!

Deferred Annuities

If you're already maximizing contributions to your 401(k), IRA, and HSA, you might be wondering how else you can shelter your hard-earned money from taxation. After maximizing those three accounts, your options become significantly more limited. However, annuities provide tax-deferred growth. You can purchase "qualified" annuities with pre-tax dollars. In general, these annuities are not as preferable as investing wisely in your 401(k). Hence, we won't discuss this type. Non-qualified deferred annuities are in addition to your 401(k) and IRA. The issue with these types of annuities is that they are legally quite complicated. To better understand what deferred annuities are, we must first define what an annuity is.

Annuity: Historically, A "Pension-Like" Insurance Contract

An annuity is effectively an insurance contract. You are provided some form of guaranteed income for life (with survivorship benefits, if desired) in exchange for an upfront policy cost. For example, an insurance company might offer a plan in which you receive $8,000 a year for life, and it might cost $100,000 to purchase that policy. If you buy that policy at 60 and live to be 100, you will have withdrawn $320,000 from that $100,000 purchase. That's a pretty solid win. If, however, you wind up passing away at 65, then you'll only have withdrawn $40,000, and the insurance company can keep the other $60,000.

As with most insurance products, it's a numbers game. The insurance company calculates the payouts with an expected rate of return on their investments and an average life expectancy. If you exceed that life expectancy or if the market tanks, you wind up ahead. If the market roars or you pass away unexpectedly, then the insurance company will profit.

You can also buy annuities with a fixed payout period. For example, you might start taking money out at 65 and have the payments spread equally over 20 years. While this option is excellent in that you know you will receive 100% of the funds, it also means that you may run out of money once that duration finishes.

What Are Non-Qualified Deferred Annuities?

A non-qualified deferred annuity is one that allows you to invest. It acts as a hybrid between a tax-deferred investment account and a regular brokerage account. There are two phases with these annuities: the accumulation phase and the payout phase.

For non-qualified deferred annuities, the accumulation phase consists of investing after-tax money into the account. Any income that account earns is not taxed immediately. The money in that account can grow tax-free until you hit the payout phase.

The payout phase consists of receiving that money from the annuity. This payout can be in the form of guaranteed income for life. Or, it can have a fixed interval like 20 years. The choice is entirely up to you and what your provider allows.

Taxation Rules

As long as the money resides within the annuity or you are transferring from one investment to another, there will be no tax bill. Earnings in the annuity grow tax-deferred until they are taken out.

Unfortunately, variable annuities have somewhat complex tax calculations. Part of the money within the account – your contributions - has already been taxed. The government won't impose a tax on that again. However, part of the annuity has grown tax-deferred. The government does want to tax that.

What will happen is that your provider will calculate how much of the money you have withdrawn is from the taxable portion vs. the non-taxable part. You will then receive a tax receipt that you can use to file your taxes correctly for the income portion.

As a quick example, suppose you have made $1 million in after-tax contributions to the annuity over the years. The total value of the account at age 65 is $1.5 million ($500,000 in gains). You start withdrawing money. In the first year, suppose you take $150,000. Your provider might allocate that as $100,000 in contributions and $50,000 in earnings. In this scenario, you would have to pay regular income tax on $50,000 (which is a tiny bill compared to what you would have had to pay on $150,000).

Investment-Only Variable Annuities

One type of variable annuity that is very popular is the investment-only one. This type of variable annuity works effectively like a tax-deferred investment account. You can pick your investments, and once you reach 59.5, you can begin withdrawing money from the annuity. There are no guaranteed income streams or the right of survivorship. It's a straightforward, cost-efficient way to save for retirement.

Who Should Consider A Non-Qualified Deferred Annuity?

If you are already maximizing all other investment vehicles (i.e., 401(k), IRA, etc.), a non-qualified variable annuity might be right for you. It allows you to defer taxes on the growth of your money until you hit the retirement age. If you are currently making $500,000, for example, the income tax on your investment income could be quite high. By using a non-qualified deferred annuity, you can let that money grow without paying those high taxes. You can spread your earnings out over multiple years in retirement and have lower tax brackets for that income.

Since you contribute to these annuities with after-tax money, you can deposit as much money as you would like. There are no limits or other restrictions. However, if you take an early withdrawal of earnings, then the standard income tax plus a 10% penalty applies. Therefore, if you ever foresee a need to withdraw your money in the future, you would be better off keeping your money in a standard brokerage account.

Non-Qualified Deferred Annuities Are An Additional Way To Save

If you are already maximizing your other retirement savings plans and need an additional way to save, you should consider opening a non-qualified deferred annuity. It is a great way to enjoy tax-deferred income growth. The investment only option makes this type of account less like a traditional "pension-like" account and more like a typical tax-deferred growth account. You can defer tax on your investment income until retirement when typically your rates will be quite a bit lower.

Long-term Care Insurance

When we are in the prime of our careers, we focus a lot on preparing for our retirement. We envision ourselves sailing around the world, going on fun adventures, and eating at all our favorite restaurants. Each of us thinks that we're going to have a fantastic time in retirement. And once that time comes, you absolutely will! If you plan right, you'll be able to bask in the sun on the beach if you want or road trip all across the country. You won't have any money concerns at all.

However, all the fun and games will eventually come to an end. As sad as that is to say, our bodies will inevitably become frailer. We'll need assistance with basic living tasks. During this time, long-term care will be necessary. That type of care might be a nursing home, or it might be some other form of assisted living. Regardless of what it is or what you call it, there's a good chance that we will all need it at some point in time. The question is: how will you pay for it?

Rising Nursing Home And Assisted Living Costs

Right now, the average cost for a private nursing home room exceeds $100,000. Even if you have $2,000,000 saved in a tax-free vehicle (like a Roth 401(k)) for your retirement, at a 5% return, all of your investment income will be going to pay for your room in the nursing home.

That figure doesn't even include other medical expenses or day-to-day living like entertainment or food. Nursing homes are expensive.

Many people might think that they can avoid some of these egregious costs by staying in their properties. After all, surely a home health aide cannot be $100,000, right? While it is true that these aides are cheaper, they're still pricey at an average cost of $50,000 per year. Since you are still living in your home, you're always looking at the property taxes and general upkeep costs of your house as well.

As we age, we expect our expenses to decrease. While they likely will drop at the start of our retirement years, there will come the point in time when they will dramatically rise again. Having to pay for some help during your life is virtually guaranteed.

How Can You Protect Against These Costs?

Even if you have done everything right by saving, opening up 401(k)s, IRAs, and HSAs, you still could have significant long-term care expenses when you age. Unless you are ultra-wealthy and $100,000 per year is easily affordable for you, you may wish to consider alternatives.

One of the best ways to protect against long-term care expenses is to purchase long term care insurance. Many people buy these plans in their 50s or 60s. The key is that you need to buy the insurance plan early. Much like other insurance plans, you cannot buy it once you already have a debilitating condition.

These plans work much like other insurance premiums. You pay specific amounts each year or month, and if you ever need long-term care, the policy will cover the payments for you. It's that simple!

I Have Health Insurance. Doesn't That Count?

No, unfortunately, most health insurance plans don't cover the cost of long-term care. Medicaid, Medicare, and various state-run programs also don't do much to cover the cost of long-term care. Even if you have health insurance, you're still going to need to brace yourself for the potential expense of long-term care.

This added expense is partly why health care becomes so costly during retirement. Not only do you potentially have out-of-pocket health costs and premiums you need to pay for (since you're no longer working), but you also have the looming expenses of some form of assisted living. For even well-prepared individuals and couples, these expenses can become overwhelming.

The Good News Is That Insurance Premiums Are Tax-Deductible

One of the other benefits of buying a long-term care insurance policy is that a portion of the premiums is tax-deductible (you have to itemize your deductions to receive this). If you are 40 or under, the deductible portion is $420 annually. This figure rises, however, as you become older. After 70, $5,220 is deductible annually. If you find that you require long-term care, it's an excellent tax-sheltered way of paying for that care, instead of needing to pay $100,000 or so every year.

When Do These Plans Pay Out?

Typically, these plans pay for your long-term care when you can no longer do a couple of basic living tasks. If you can no longer do two activities like bathing, dressing, eating, transferring yourself in or out of bed, getting on or off the toilet, or caring for incontinence, then these plans will pay for your long-term care.

Of course, the insurance company will need to review your medical history to determine if you are eligible to receive funds for your assisted living or not. The insurance company may also send out a representative or a nurse to evaluate your physical condition to process your claim.

Many policies have an "elimination period." This interval can be 30, 60, or 90 days. During this time, you will need to pay for your long-term care. After this timeframe passes, the insurance company will pay for the rest. The idea behind this period is that the insurance company should only pay for care that requires a significant duration, not for two weeks, for example, that you needed to be in an assisted living facility.

Buy Long-Term Care Insurance Now

Long-term care insurance is a fantastic tax-deductible way to plan for assisted living. While you may be lucky and never need a nursing home, there's an equally good possibility that you will require one when you get older. Approximately 15% of older adults require 5+ years of extended care. While the odds are in your favor that you won't need long-term care for a substantial time, it can be financially devastating if you do. Protect your hard-earned wealthy by purchasing long-term care insurance sooner rather than later!

What To Do With Social Security In Retirement

If you are a high net worth individual, you likely have two financial characteristics. First, you probably have healthy retirement savings accounts that can support you once you decide to give up working. Second, you probably are maximizing your working contributions to Social Security.

The maximum monthly benefit that people can receive from Social Security as of 2020 is $3,790. That figure assumes someone files for it at age 70. If you file at age 62, that figure drops to $2,265.

For individuals who have spent their life maximizing 401(k)s, IRAs, and other tax-advantaged accounts, this extra income, while helpful, is not needed for day-to-day expenses. It's excess and, as such, should be used in a way that is advantageous tax-wise.

Social Security Taxes Are Different Than Regular Income Taxes

First, it's worth noting that tax on social security income is different than that on your ordinary income. You add half of your social security income to your regular taxable income. You will have to pay income tax on 50% of your benefits if your taxable income is between $25,000 and $34,000. Below $25,000, the government levies no taxes.

Above $34,000, you will pay your standard income tax rate on 85% of your benefits. Those brackets rise to $32,000 and $44,000, respectively, for married couples.

Most high net worth individuals will be in a position to receive at least $44,000 in income from retirement accounts. Given that only 50% of your social security amounts are subject to taxation, social security in and of itself will never be enough to make you pay tax ($45,480 * 50% = $22,740, which is less than $25,000 threshold for single filers). Therefore, generally, what you will want to do is minimize your taxable income during retirement so you can keep as much of your social security benefit tax-free.

Withdraw From Roth IRAs In Conjunction With Social Security Payments

Distributions from Roth accounts - both Roth 401(k)s and Roth IRAs - are not considered as taxable income. If you have $200,000, for example, in your Roth IRA, you can withdraw from that first to minimize your tax on social security. For example, if you take your social security at age 62 as an individual, you will receive $27,180 per year. This amount means that only $2,180 annually will be subject to 50% of your regular income tax bracket. You can supplement that $2,265 per month with Roth withdrawals, so you pay as little tax as possible on the income.

Note that, generally, you will want to wait as long as possible before drawing from social security. If you take withdrawals at 62 and live to 90, you will receive $761,040 in social security benefits (not accounting for annual increases), and most of that money will be tax-free. If you wait until 70, you'll receive $909,600 worth of benefits, and all that money will still be tax-free, so long as you keep your taxable income to a minimum. Since Roth IRA withdrawals are not taxable, withdrawing from your Roth account keeps your social security payments away from the hands of the IRS.

Withdraw From Taxable Funds First

The second method of minimizing tax is a logical extension of the first one. Withdraw tax-deferred income first and then use your Roth accounts when you hit 70 (and start bringing in social security).

As a simplified example, suppose you have $1,000,000 in a taxable 401(k) and $1,000,000 in a Roth IRA. If you want to retire at age 65, draw $200,000 per year from your taxable 401(k). After taxes, you might take home something along the lines of $140,000. Then, once you hit 70, you can start your social security benefits at $45,480 per year. You can also withdraw $100,000 per year from your Roth IRA. Your combined returns are now $145,480, and none of that is subject to tax. Assuming standard rates of returns, you can last for 12 years using the funds from your Roth IRA combined with social security.

By sequencing your withdrawals correctly, you can take the taxable equivalent of $200,000 per year for 17 years off of $2 million in savings!

Avoid Required Minimum Distributions

Depending on how much you have saved in taxable accounts, you may run into the issue of required minimum distributions. After 70.5 years old, the government mandates that you take a portion of your 401(k) and other tax-deferred accounts per year.

You can sometimes avoid these distributions by purchasing a qualified longevity annuity contract. If purchased with retirement funds, required minimum distributions will not need to happen until the date at which the annuity starts.

For example, let's say you have $500,000 in your 401(k) left at age 70.5, and you want to live off your Roth and Social Security for ten years. You can buy one of these contracts to defer a percentage of that 401(k) income tax until you hit 85 (or an age that is earlier, if you want). You can then work on drawing down the Roth accounts and defer taxes on the other retirement income further. It's a strategy that can work, but generally, you would want to consult with a financial advisor before buying anything.

Minimizing Tax on Social Security Benefits: It Can Be Done

The best way to minimize the tax you pay on Social Security payments is to structure your retirement withdrawals with Social Security in mind. Use your taxable income first so you can delay starting your Social Security benefits. Then seek to use your Roth funds in combination with Social Security to minimize overall taxation. If you are receiving the maximum distribution of $45,480, that is a relatively sizeable tax-free sum of money each year. When combined with your Roth accounts, you can receive a significant amount of money tax-free each year.

Other situations, like the qualified longevity annuity contract, require more in-depth, personalized financial planning that only a qualified financial advisor can give.

The key takeaway is that, if structured right, you can maximize your returns from Social Security by minimizing taxation. At the maximum rates, Social Security makes a nice tax-free bonus each year!

C Corporation Tax Advantages

It might seem strange to think of opening up a C corporation if you're not looking to become an entrepreneur. Most people think of opening a company as being a significant endeavor. You need to file paperwork with the state, get a business account, and then you need to do something useful with that business. Maybe you're looking to operate a consultancy, or perhaps you're writing software for clients. People usually think of C corporations as being very active businesses.

However, sometimes, C corporations are used to minimize tax obligations for their owners. Frequently, it's often more beneficial in terms of taxation to be the sole shareholder of a C corporation for other income streams as opposed to receiving that income directly. For more on how that works, keep on reading!

First, A Company Primer

You have likely seen the term LLC before. If you've been looking into starting your own business, you've also probably seen the words "S corporation" and "C corporation." Each of these structures is different.

An LLC (limited liability company) is the quickest way to form a company. There is no board of directors, and it cannot issue shares. Since there isn't a board of directors, there are no annual meetings that need to happen. There is very little paperwork involved with an LLC. It is considered to be a pass-through entity by the IRS. Any income you make via the LLC flows through to you and is put directly on your Schedule C of your 1040, like a sole proprietorship.

Both the S and C corporations are actual corporations registered with the state (so both can be Acme Corporation, for example). Since they are corporations, they typically need a board of directors and to have annual meetings. The difference between the two is in how they are taxed. An S corporation's taxes treat it like a pass-through entity. It does not file a tax return. All profits and losses flow through to the owners (much like a sole proprietorship). A C corporation is the more traditional corporate structure. It is an entity of itself and files a tax return. The corporation can issue stock, grant dividends, pay employees, and so on.

Why A C Corporation For Tax Benefits?

Since sole proprietorships, S corporations, and LLCs are all pass-through entities, the government will tax any income you make with these businesses at your regular income tax rate. It goes on your Schedule C, and there are minimal tax savings.

On the other hand, since a C corporation is a separate entity, it enjoys significant tax benefits. Note that your C corporation does not to be a physical storefront or anything like that. You can use your C corporation to enjoy tax benefits for rental income, investment income, and other sources that you obtain outside of your standard employment. As long as you maintain a proper set of

C Corporation Tax Advantages

books for the company and treat it as independent, the IRS and courts will view the corporation as legitimate.

The first and most obvious benefit of having a C corporation is that the Tax Cuts and Jobs Act of 2017 changed the C corporation tax rate to be a flat 21%. Conversely, the top tax rate for an individual is 37%. By having money flow through your company, you can let some of it grow at a reduced tax rate.

Second, any expenses that you pay are also tax-deductible. If your business owns properties and you are obtaining rental income, then any cost related to those properties is deductible. You can also count employee payments and benefits as expenses as well, thereby reducing your company's taxable income.

There Are Less Obvious Benefits As Well

Your corporation can deduct 100% of certain fringe benefits. These include health plans, long-term care, and disability insurance. If you find yourself in a situation in which you want or need additional fringe benefits, you may find that you can use the income from your C corporation to fund them via pre-tax dollars.

If you give to charity, a C corporation can write off 10% its taxable income as a business expense. You can carry over these donations for the next five years, as well.

You can also use your C corporation to fund retirement programs. A great example of this is the SEP IRA. This IRS treats funds allocated for this program as a business expense for the employer. In 2019, you can contribute a maximum of 25% of the employee's annual income, or $56,000 per person. These contributions stack with other plans, such as HSAs, 401(k)s, and so on. That means, in theory, you could defer tax on $30,000 or so between HSAs, 401(k)s, and IRAs and have your company contribute $56,000 tax-free towards your retirement. If done right, you can defer taxation on a significant amount of money.

A Note On Closely-Held Corporations

If your company is a closely-held corporation (that is, you or your family is the sole owner of it), then it is subject to specific rules and regulations that sometimes affect the eligibility for some of these tax benefits. For example, if your company is closely-held and earns most of its income via passive sources, then it can be subject to a tax penalty.

Therefore, before setting up a C corporation for tax benefits, you should consult with a qualified financial specialist and attorney to make sure your plans won't cause issues down the road.

A Second Entity Helps With Tax Deferral

Whether you have employment at a company or you are a professional looking for tax advantages, having a C corporation can help you reduce your tax liability. You can pay for fringe benefits with pre-tax dollars as opposed to post-tax ones. You can also adjust how much you take out of the company and when. There are retirement plans (like the SEP IRA) that are available to increase your tax-deferred retirement contributions. Setting up a C corporation is not trivial, but under the right circumstances, it can provide significant tax advantages.

There Are Two Additional Advantages!

There are two additional benefits for C corporations. The first benefit is called COLI (corporate-owned life insurance), and the second benefit is DRD (dividends received deduction). In this post, we'll take a look at these two benefits and some scenarios in which they might be useful to shelter some of your income from extra taxation.

Corporate-Owned Life Insurance: What Is It?

Many people, including small business owners, are not familiar with the term "corporate-owned life insurance." Essentially, this term means what it says. A company purchases a life insurance policy on one or more key employees. In effect, this policy is no different than other insurance policies (it pays out when the employee passes away), however the fact that the company owns the insurance policy has some uniquely beneficial properties.

The original intent behind corporate-owned life insurance policies was to provide insurance if critical people were to pass away. For example, Apple may have wanted to take a COLI policy on Steve Jobs or Microsoft may have wanted one on Bill Gates. If a visionary founder passes away, a company might be in big trouble. While you may not have a business the size of Apple or Microsoft, there's no doubt that your business has key people, such as yourself, that keep it afloat.

If your family relies on your business income to live, then your passing away might have many repercussions. Not only will they lose your income, but they will also potentially have issues running the business. A corporate-owned life insurance policy infuses the company with cash in a situation like this so it can stay afloat until other family members can run it or until they can sell it.

Of course, this policy is not just for owners and founders - any employee can be on the life insurance plan! Even if they leave the company, they can still be on the COLI, and the company can collect when they pass away in the future.

Benefits Of COLI

COLI is conceptually simple, but the benefits it imparts are not immediately apparent. It has two primary uses. The first is for a small business that wants to ensure that the unexpected loss of a key employee does not irreparably damage the company. The second is for more prominent corporations that use COLI to hedge against future benefit payments for crucial talent.

Executive benefits, like non-qualified deferred compensation plans, cost substantial money. COLI is a

C Corporation Tax Advantages

way to hedge against those costs. Once you obtain a corporate-owned life insurance policy, there are three main benefits. First, gains on policy cash value are tax-deferred. Second, you can gain access to cash values through withdrawals and loans. This money can fund plan distributions for crucial talent. Finally, reallocating assets in the policy doesn't trigger any tax event.

If you own your own business and looking to buy a COLI plan, speak with a financial advisor today to make sure it is right for you and your business.

Dividends Received Deduction

You can shelter some of your taxes on dividends by using a C corporation. As per IRS regulations, a C corporation can deduct 70% of any dividend payment it receives from another company it owns. If the company owns more than 20% of the company, that percentage rises to 80%. If they own more than 80% of the corporation, then the deductible percentage increases to a full 100%.

In effect, this means that you will likely pay less on dividends received through investments that your C corporation owns as opposed to ones you own personally. The personal dividend tax rate ranges from 15% to 20%. However, the tax rate for corporations is now 21%, and you can deduct 70% of the dividend amount.

If you receive a dividend of $100 from company A in your brokerage account, you will owe $15 to $20 in taxes. However, if Your Co. owns company A and receives that same $100 dividend, then it will pay $6.30. Why? Your company can deduct 70% of the dividend value. It then pays 21% of the remaining $30, which equals $6.30. By having your corporation own the shares, you reduce your tax liability.

Multiple Benefits Of Owning A C Corporation

If your primary source of income comes from a business that you own, you may wish to see if purchasing a corporate-owned life insurance policy can benefit your business. Furthermore, you'll also want to take a look at the DRD and see if receiving dividends through your corporation can help you shelter some income from taxation.

Given how cheap companies are to open, high-income individuals should consult with a tax professional and financial planner to see if there are benefits to having one - even if it's just for tax purposes. It can often be useful to have a separate legal entity to put income through so that it can be taxed lower. A great example of this is how a high-income individual can combine a regular 401(k) with a SEP to maximize tax benefits.

However, please keep in mind that corporate tax laws tend to be complicated, and bookkeeping for a corporation can be difficult. You should consult with a lawyer, accountant, and financial planner to ensure that any tax-deferral opportunities you would like to take advantage of will be 100% legal and will withstand any IRS scrutiny.

Dynasty Trusts: What They Are And Why You Might Need Them

When discussing ways to shelter income and assets from taxation, most people think of income taxes. 401(k)s, IRAs, and other investment vehicles work by protecting your income and assets from taxation until you retire. These are fantastic savings mechanisms that everyone should employ. However, less talked about is a more insidious double taxation that all wealthy families have to deal with eventually - gift and estate taxes. The money that you have worked so hard to earn and preserve will wind up taxed again once it gets passed along to your heirs. The estate tax rate can be as high as 40% if you wind up hitting the top bracket.

Imagine thinking that your loved ones will inherit your estate, only to have it slashed nearly in half by Uncle Sam. For individuals with a high net worth, proper estate planning is essential. Whether you are presently in retirement and looking at how to minimize taxes your heirs will pay, or you are an executive who expects to be in this situation in the future, you must plan now to reduce estate taxes.

A Brief Description Of The Often Misunderstood Estate And Gift Tax

The estate and gift tax laws are some of the most nuanced and misunderstood ones in the IRS tax code. The origins of the estate tax can be traced back to 1916. When originally enacted, the exemption was $50,000 (which was quite a bit of money over 100 years ago). Since then, the exclusion amount has risen to $11.4 million. If you leave more than $11.4 million to your heirs, your heirs will need to pay a very steep tax rate.

For estates above $11.4 million, there is a graduated tax rate. For estates exceeding the exclusion amount by $1,000,000 or more, they will owe $345,800 in taxes on the first million plus 40% for every dollar after that. As a quick example, if your estate is $20 million, your heirs will have the first $11.4 million excluded. They will owe tax on the remaining $8.6 million, to the tune of $3,385,800 (or 17% of your total estate). These figures assume a single person is passing their estate to their descendants. If you are married, then the amount you can give to your loved ones doubles to $22.8 million.

If you think that's too much money to give the government for a "death tax," then you should know that there are ways to help minimize the burden your loved ones will experience in the future.

Dynasty Trusts

One way to help bypass these egregious taxes is to form a dynasty trust. A standard trust works by creating a separate entity in which you transfer your assets. These must be irrevocable trusts. That means that you will no longer have control over the assets. The trustee will possess them and will be contractually obligated to distribute them at a later time. If you use a revocable trust, then the assets are technically within your control and can be subject to the estate and gift taxes.

A dynasty trust is very similar, except that it is structured to be cross-generational. The goal of the dynasty trust is to preserve your wealth across generations (not just your children, but their children and grandchildren as well). A dynasty trust is useful for families looking to protect intergenerational wealth and shelter it from taxation.

A critical aspect of the estate tax is that it not only affects your immediate heirs, but it also affects their direct heirs as well. When your heirs are subject to the estate tax, they will have less than they can pass on to their heirs, and so on. A striking whitepaper by RBC Wealth Management showed how the estate tax could make the difference between your great-grandchildren inheriting $50 million via regular estate channels and $231 million with a dynasty trust.

In short, if you want to preserve your wealth, for multiple generations, you're going to want to set up a dynasty trust!

How Do I Set Up One Of These Trusts?

Since you are dealing with significant values of money, you should consult with a lawyer and financial professional to ensure that you are setting up the trust in such a way that it will have the tax benefits you seek. With that said, the first step to setting up a dynasty trust is to create one in a state that allows the trust to exist in perpetuity. Some states have rules that require these entities to end 21 years after the death of the original grantor. Other US states, like California, set the maximum duration at 90 years. Delaware and Florida, for example, allow trusts that last forever. You will need to work with your lawyer and financial planner to ensure that your new financial trust will have the legal properties that you want.

You will also want to set up an irrevocable trust. Part of the requirement to exclude this money from estate taxes is that you must no longer have control over these funds. If you do have control over them, then they will wind up being part of your estate and subject to the very tax that you were trying to avoid.

Finally, trusts are subject to income tax. If you put bonds and such in these trusts that earn taxable income, income taxes will be due. Generally, people fund these tax protection entities with stocks that don't pay dividends or tax-free municipal bonds. Of course, what you decide to put in there is your decision, but, again, your financial planner can help you pick assets that will preserve your wealth better for future generations.

Dynasty Trusts: An Option To Explore For Multi-Generational Wealth

If you have an estate that will be subject to the estate tax or if you expect to be in this situation, you should explore a dynasty trust to preserve that wealth for generations. With estate taxes being incredibly high, you can leave your loved ones best prepared by planning a little bit now to avoid substantial tax bills for your heirs in the future!

Other Trust Types, Including ILIT and Crummey

The world of financial trusts is often confusing and can be challenging to understand. Part of the confusion over trusts stems from the fact that there are so many different varieties. If you look at trusts, there are five primary trust types. There are living trusts, revocable ones, irrevocable, testamentary, and funded or unfunded. However, those aren't the only types. Dozens of other types may or may not be beneficial to your generational wealth objectives depending on your potential life circumstances.

If you are wondering what all the trust types are, you're not alone. Many wealthy individuals receive advice to open a trust when talking with their financial advisors. If you are looking at trusts, there are two types you will want to know about: the irrevocable life insurance trust (ILIT) and the Crummey trust.

Irrevocable Life Insurance Trust

An irrevocable life insurance trust (ILIT) is a trust type that is popular for many wealthy families. As the name implies, ILITs cannot be modified, rescinded, or amended once created. The original owner cannot cancel the trust or get any of the assets back. Therefore, people should take great care in constructing these trusts to ensure that they adequately reflect the wishes of the owner.

As the name also implies, the trust's principal asset is a life insurance policy. Upon death, the trust fiduciaries will pay out the proceeds of the insurance policy following the trust rules.

Why Use An ILIT?

Conceptually, an ILIT is reasonably straightforward. It's a life insurance policy owned by a third-party who then distributes the policy's proceeds upon death. However, the ILIT has significant hidden benefits that make it useful for not just wealthy families, but even upper or middle-class ones as well.

First, the death benefits paid via the life insurance policy from an ILIT will not be part of the estate for income tax purposes. Currently, the federal gift exemption sits at approximately $12,000,000. While many estates are not that large, those are federal rules. State laws sometimes tax estates starting at $1 or $2 million. Even if your state presently does not have an estate tax, it may have one in the future, requiring a strategy to avoid it. For example, even though it didn't pass, California was going to tax estates at 40% above $3.5 million.

Many people can unknowingly hit these state limits. For example, many homes in California are worth $2 million or more. If you had a life insurance policy, plus a home, plus retirement accounts, you could have triggered a significant estate tax unwittingly.

An ILIT places the life insurance part of the inheritance under someone else's control. As such, it is not part of the estate. Therefore, your heirs will not have taxation on this benefit.

Furthermore, a trust can also have rules about distribution. If you want to ensure your relatives do not squander their payouts, you can set regulations when and how beneficiaries will receive their money. For example, you might have a $1 million benefit, and you might set the distribution schedule to be $100,000 over ten years.

Crummey Trust

Despite the name, Crummey trusts are not a real trust type. The term "Crummey trust" refers to a trust with the Crummey provision. The name for this provision comes from the last name of the first person to execute this idea successfully.

The way this provision works is conceptually simple. Usually, gifts are subject to the gift tax (if they are above $15,000 for an individual and $30,000 for a married couple). If you are a married couple funding a trust for 30 years, you could exclude $900,000 from gift taxation.

The issue is that gifts qualify for the exclusion only if the recipient has a present interest. This term means that they must be able to make use of the gift immediately. A gift to an irrevocable trust (like the ILIT type discussed above) doesn't meet this present interest qualification. Therefore, the entire amount is subject to the gift tax.

A Crummey provision permits the trust's beneficiary to withdraw the gift to the trust for some time, typically 30 days. A parent can contribute money to a trust designated for their child, and the child has the option to withdraw the funds for 30 days after.

Assuming they don't withdraw the money, the funds remain in the irrevocable trust. By giving them the option to remove the funds for some duration after deposit, they now have a "present interest" in the gift. Therefore the entire deposit qualifies for the gift exemption of $15,000 for an individual or $30,000 for a married couple. In other words, you can now have those sums of money not count towards the gift limits and tax.

If you are planning on funding an irrevocable trust over many years, these exemptions add up significantly. The trust still has all the same usual provisions. You get to exclude some of the contributions from the gift tax.

Find The Right Trust Type For You

There are many types of trusts, and finding the right one for you can be challenging. Some trust types and provisions make immediate logical sense. The Crummey provision is one of those things. It's hard to argue against having a portion of your gift excluded from the gift tax. The ILIT is also another example of a trust type that makes immediate and undeniable sense. Having life insurance benefits excluded from estate tax means your heirs can enjoy more of the funds. The exclusion also benefits them if they face an unexpected tax bill - they can use the life insurance proceeds to pay that bill!

However, no trust is one-size-fits-all. Families should tailor each trust to their own needs. Fortunately, there are many estate and financial planners that know the ins-and-outs of each of these trusts. If you are looking at leaving money and property to your children, you should consider the value of your estate and plan accordingly. The last thing your heirs should have to deal with when you pass away is the taxman!

Which Tax-Advantaged Accounts Should I Open First?

The IRS code permits many types of tax-advantaged accounts. From traditional IRAs to 401(k)s to Roth accounts to HSAs, the law has many three to four-letter acronyms that help you shelter some of your income from taxation. Many of these accounts you are familiar with because they are a part of everyday life. For example, many employers offer 401(k)s, so you have likely seen how they work. Other investment vehicles, like non-qualified deferred compensation plans, are more obscure. You will have probably only seen these if you are a C-level executive.

With so many accounts to choose from, it's hard to know where to start? What account should you invest in first? What investments should you explore once you are maximizing your deductions in the standard accounts? These are the questions we'll answer in the following few paragraphs!

An Explanation Of Different Tax Advantages

Tax-advantaged accounts come in three types: completely tax-free, tax-deductible contributions, and tax-free withdrawals. Completely tax-free accounts have no taxation whatsoever. You can contribute to them without paying income tax on the money, they grow without any taxation, and you can withdraw from them without paying income tax. This type of account is the best for obvious reasons. The second type of account is the tax-deductible one. A tax-deductible account lets you contribute pre-tax money and allows the funds to grow without taxation. You will have to pay Uncle Sam once you withdraw, however. Finally, a tax-free withdrawal account lets you make after-tax contributions. Those contributions grow tax-free, and then the funds can be taken out without taxation.

The completely tax-free account style is the best. It bypasses taxation altogether. Whether or not you want a tax-deductible or tax-free withdrawal account depends on what you expect your tax rate to be during retirement. If you plan to have a lower tax rate, you want a tax-deductible account. If you expect to have a higher tax rate, then you want a tax-free withdrawal one.

You Need Liquidity

Before investing in any tax-advantaged account, first, ensure that you have adequate liquidity. Most of these accounts have penalties for early withdrawals. The IRS will usually levy a 10% or 20% penalty for taking the money out before age 59.5. If you think there is any way you might need the money before that age, do not invest it.

While guidelines vary, the general recommendation is to have six months of living expenses saved. You'd typically want one month's worth of expenses as cash or a cash equivalent. Then, you'd like to have 5-6 months of expenses in stocks, bonds, and other higher-interest bearing account types.

First, Maximize Your HSA, If You Have One

The health savings account is the only wholly tax-free account. With the HSA, you can contribute pre-tax money. That money is free to grow unencumbered by taxation. Then, as long as you use the funds for qualified medical expenses, you can withdraw it for those expenses tax-free. Any money you contribute to your HSA bypasses taxation completely.

The maximum contribution you can make to an HSA is $7,000. Some people are hesitant to contribute to these plans because they do not foresee any immediate medical bills. However, these accounts can keep growing in value until you need them. Eventually, you will have medical costs, and this money can pay those bills without taxation.

Second, Contribute To Your 401(k) Or Similar Plan

Assuming your employer has a 401(k) or similar plan (like a 403(b)), the next account you will want to contribute to is that plan. Whether or not you make Roth contributions or traditional ones is up to you, but regardless of what you add, you'll want to be a part of your employer's plan. There are a couple of reasons for this, but the primary one is that employers will often match 401(k) contributions. Some employers will match 50 cents on the dollar. Others will match dollar for dollar up to 6%. Every company is different, but your next priority (after the HSA) is to get that match!

Third, Open An IRA (For Both You And Your Spouse, If You Have One)

Next, you will want to open an IRA. If you are married, you can contribute to your spouse's IRA as well, so you can shelter additional income that way. An IRA is self-directed, so you will have access to any investments that you want. Typically, you'll want to opt for a traditional IRA, which provides you a tax deduction for contributions, but all withdrawals after 59.5 are subject to income tax.

Fourth, Open A 529 Plan

There is a good chance that you know someone who wants to go to school. Whether you have children who will be requiring money for educational expenses or you're planning on going back to college at some point in time, a 529 plan is the best way to pay for those costs. Contributions consist of after-tax money, but any income your 529 earns is tax-free if you use it on qualified educational expenses. The definition of qualified is also relatively loose. Most costs qualify, including private K-12 costs, college tuition, books, supplies, and so on. A 529 plan is the best way to save for school!

Fifth, Everything Else

Once you have your HSA funded, your 401(k) maxed out, your IRA maxed out, and enough money going into your 529 to pay for your expected education expenses, then you're going to want to look at other ways to save money. The backdoor Roth IRA and mega backdoor Roth are good next steps. If your company allows it, you can take a look at setting up a non-qualified deferred compensation plan to defer taxation on some of your income until rates are lower. You'll also want to take a look at minimizing estate taxes through a trust or dynasty trust.

There Are Many Options For Reducing Your Tax Burden

Reducing your tax burden is possible through some of these investment vehicles. Pick the right ones for you to keep as much as possible of your hard-earned money to yourself!

2020 Tax Law Changes You Need To Know

Many changes will be coming for retirement savers in 2020. Most of these changes are positive ones, aimed at encouraging more saving and reducing the number of penalties that people face for withdrawals.

In case you missed it with all the recent news, Congress passed a retirement savings bill called the SECURE Act, which was part of the legislation to avoid a government shutdown in late 2019. The SECURE Act is incredibly lengthy at 1,773 words, but it deals with improving retirement savings for people from all walks of life. Whether you're making $20,000 a year, $200,000, or $2 million, you'll want to know about these changes and how they will impact your retirement planning.

Contribution Limits Changing

The maximum contribution amounts for many popular account types are increasing. Workers may now contribute $19,500 to their 401(k) accounts. This figure is up from $19,000 in 2019. Catch-up contribution limits have also increased by the same amount and are now $6,500 instead of $6,000. IRA limits have remained the same at $6,000.

If you are maximizing your IRA and 401(k) contributions, you will be able to defer tax on $25,500 worth of income in 2020. If you can take advantage of catch-up contributions, you'll be able to defer tax on $31,500 of your income.

Required Minimum Distribution Age Increasing

Previously, if you had a tax-deferred retirement account like a 401(k) or an IRA, you had to take minimum distributions when you turned 70.5 years old. Even if you had enough money in other savings to live, you still would have to take money out of your tax-deferred account. Of course, you would have to pay taxes on that money at the time of distribution.

The new law increases that age to 72, so you now have an extra 1.5 years before you need to start taking minimum distributions. Assuming you have enough in other retirement accounts to live, this change enables your money to grow tax-deferred for longer.

Note that this law only applies to those turning 70.5 after December 31, 2019. If you became 70.5 in 2019, you must still comply with the existing rules and regulations. In other words, you still need to take the required minimum distributions.

IRA Contribution Rules Are Changing

Previously, persons aged 70.5 and above could not contribute to an IRA. Congress removed this prohibition. As long as you earn income, you can contribute to an IRA using that income! You can continue to defer taxation on $6,000 of your investment or business income for as long as you live. This rule change is fantastic for entrepreneurs and professionals who elect to work into their 70s and 80s.

Inheritance Rules Are Also Changing

Inherited retirement accounts have historically been able to distribute assets over the beneficiary's lifetime. In other words, if you inherit a 401(k) from your parents, you don't need to withdraw money from those assets immediately. You can defer taxation and let the funds continue to grow over your lifetime.

Under the new law, inherited retirement accounts must distribute funds over ten years. There are some exemptions to this rule (spouses, minor children, etc.). However, there aren't many exceptions. If you are looking at estate planning, you'll want to keep this change in mind.

If you have already inherited an account, please note that this rule only applies to future account inheritances. Your currently inherited account will continue to behave as usual.

401(k) Plans Can Now More Easily Offer Annuities

403(b) plans offer annuities most often. The recent law changes make it easier for 401(k) plans to join the annuity club. Your employer or provider needn't offer them. However, they are more likely to do so with these changes.

Of course, if you are self-employed and have a 401(k) plan through your own business, you can choose to offer annuities to yourself if that is of interest to you.

Repay Student Loans With 529 Funds

If you have student loans, you can use 529 savings to repay those up to $10,000 worth. Bear in mind, though, that there is no "double-dipping." If you use your 529 plan to repay student loans, then you cannot deduct the student loan interest applicable to those payments on your tax return. This new provision is helpful for students who may have had to take a loan after exhausting their parent's 529 funds. If parents can replenish that 529 afterward, they can now pay $10,000 of their child's student loans.

Lifetime Income Disclosure

Congress included a provision to instruct the Department of Labor to investigate a new disclosure that 401(k) plan providers would be obligated to provide. This disclosure would inform participants of how they are doing on their savings goals. The hope would be that people who are behind on saving would receive these lifetime income disclosures and elect to put more of their paycheck aside.

Note that while the bill asks the Department of Labor to investigate this potential process, it doesn't mandate anything. The department will likely not finalize these disclosures until 2022 or later. However, most workers will appreciate the reminder of their savings goals and how their current savings amounts stack up.

What You Need To Do

Most of these rule changes are passive. The contribution limit increases mean that you can start contributing a little bit more to your 401(k) beginning in 2020. You might also want to start planning for the inherited account changes. If you are planning on leaving your 401(k), IRA, or other tax-sheltered accounts to your children, you may wish to see if that still makes the most sense with the distributions required within ten years.

However, for the most part, everything is business as usual. While 2020 brings some tweaks to existing accounts, there are no major surprises here. There are no new account types and no earth-shaking changes that will have significant repercussions on your savings potential. You'll be able to save a little bit more, have more choice, and be able to keep your money in your tax-deferred account for longer!

Conclusion

Hopefully this book has been beneficial for you to learn more about the account types that are available for retirement. There are numerous ones discussed, but certainly the most common are 401(k)s, IRAs, and 529s. Other retirement accounts and strategies are less common, of course, but of high value to high net worth individuals.

If you would like more information about any of these accounts or would like financial planning, please feel free to reach out to Adil Mackwani at my website:

https://mandawealth.com .

Thank you for reading this book!

Disclosure:

CONTENT

All written content in this book is for information purposes only. Opinions expressed herein are solely those of Adil Mackwani and Mackwani & Associates Wealth Management, LLC (doing business as M&A Wealth) unless otherwise specifically cited. Material presented is believed to be from reliable sources and no representations are made by our firm as to another parties' informational accuracy or completeness. All information or ideas provided should be discussed in detail with an advisor, accountant or legal counsel prior to implementation.

This book may provide links to others for the convenience of our users. Our firm has no control over the accuracy or content of these other websites.

REGISTRATION INFORMATION

Advisory services are offered through Mackwani & Associates Wealth Management, LLC; an investment advisor firm domiciled in the State of Texas doing business as M&A Wealth. The presence of this book on the Internet shall not be directly or indirectly interpreted as a solicitation of investment advisory services to persons of another jurisdiction unless otherwise permitted by statute.

Follow-up or individualized responses to consumers in a particular state by our firm in the rendering of personalized investment advice for compensation shall not be made without our first complying with jurisdiction requirements or pursuant an applicable state exemption.

For information concerning the status or disciplinary history of a broker-dealer, investment advisor, or their representatives, a consumer should contact their state securities administrator.

Notes:

Made in the USA
Middletown, DE
27 November 2020